Seasons

of the

Soul

From the coldest winter nights to the warm summer lights, these poems explore the changing seasons of the soul.

Joel George Mathew

ISBN: 978-93-341-7064-1

E ISBN: 978-93-341-5907-3

In Loving Memory of My Father

Itty George Iype

Dedication

To my dear father, who I wish could read this.

To my mother, who believed in me, supported me, nurtured my skills, and painstakingly compiled all my works together.

To my sister Neethi, who is always there for me; even in my darkest days, she would pave a path for me out of the forest of despair. She always proofreads my works and makes suggestions that improve upon the original, transmuting bronze into gold.

To my sister, Thrupthi, who helped me with the book cover and formatting.

To Johann, who pushed me to put pen to paper and publish this work.

To my brother and sister-in-law, who always provide moral and spiritual support.

To my two little nieces who light up my gloomy world.

To all my dear friends and families that have supported and been there for me.

Last but not least, thank you for taking the time to read this book. Now let's embark on an adventurous journey.

Contents

Foreword

As Joel's cousin and close confidante, I've had the privilege of witnessing his literary growth. His passion for poetry has always impressed me. This collection showcases his unique voice, tackling themes related to love, fear, hope, and darkness. His writing is both accessible and profound.

Joel and I spent our early formative years together in our maternal grandparents' home in Kerala. I remember being a beaming big sister when he was brought home after he was born. Since we were the youngest among the four cousins, born just 3 years apart, our bond has always been special.

Later in our school years and beyond, we would meet up during vacations and compare our respective tastes in fantasy literature. Joel's mother, my aunt, would proudly show his poems and songs to close relatives, including me. Not being talented in writing poetry myself, I was fascinated by how he was able to weave a song through his words. Some of his poems have even been selected as lyrics for Bible camp theme songs.

Joel's father tragically passed away after a long illness while he was still in high school. Since they were very close, that brought a marked change to his psyche. He turned his pain inward, and writing became his outlet while he shut himself away from the world. Many poems from this collection portray the raw emotions that he experienced during those dark times.

Over the last decade as Joel has been healing, his poems have also reflected the shift. This book has captured the essence of his soul, and I'm sure all his readers will be moved as they journey with him.

Neethi Sarah John

A Long Cold Winter

It's the dead of winter. The chilling winds of despair freeze you to your bones. You have nothing but a worn-out winter coat of hope to shield you from the icy grip of despair. Away from your home and hearth, you can only hope the comforting days of spring roll by, bringing songs of hope with it. It's a long and cold winter night, but it won't last forever.

Solemn Symphony of a Soul

Listen to my silence,

It sings a sweet melody

Watch the tunes dance,

To the sound of my threnody.

I hold my eyes up high,

So I can watch the sky.

The silence of the night

Slowly mask the cries.

Six feet down he lays,

Under the solemn moon.

Crimson are these hands,

As I lie in my new grave.

The Ghost of Empires Past

The night sings a strange dark dirge.

In the street roams a plagueful scourge.

The wind whispers secrets of a fall,

Of an empire now veiled in dark pall.

The moon hides her light,

From this city once so bright.

Once adorned with cosmic gold,

Now a withered meadow, grey and cold.

A city of decay where the dead coalesce,

A place where the Grim finds his solace.

But this land be not devoid of life

For through these meadows black,

Roams a maiden bright.

Where falls her feet, all shadows flee,

Where falls her shadow, all wraiths flee

No demon's clutch or angel's touch,

But the ghost of an empire on endless watch.

Through the ruins she doth roam,

A desolate place that she calls home.

A guardian of empires past,

Or harbinger of end times forecast,

With her shroud of dismay,

All she has to say,

"Fall not into hubris,

For what follows is the abyss."

Moonlight Ballet

She dances away,

In the pale moonlit stage,

She dances through the pain,

Of the piercing blade.

She dances away,

Her last ballet,

Death, behold her final play,

The end of her moonlight daze.

She danced away,

Her final dance,

An ode to death,

A reverence for life.

A Cold Summer Mourning

The warm sun gleams from above,

Upon her rosy cheeks on mount below.

The weather so bright and warm,

Yet her skin so pale and cold.

A Friday cheer and a warm summer morn,

Yet a soul sleeps here with no one to mourn.

In the streets she sleeps, all alone,

Surrounded by suits of a morning crowd.

She held in her hands a fist full of hope,

A hope snuffed out, now left is despair.

Her dreams snuffed out, now just a Jane,

Will no one cry for this deceased dame?

A scene so sad, it brings me to tears,

But eases my heart with her peaceful smile.

Here lies the dame of a cold summer morn,

A Jane no more, for I name her Hope.

Forest of Despair

In this forest, away from light of the sun,

I run with eager breath into the deep, away from peace,

Where trees of desolation take root,

The fruit of thorny, twisted thoughts, dark in colour,

Here flows a river, a river named Misery.

Deep in reverie, I find a fallen kingdom.

Away from light and fortune's wisdom.

In the midst of looming dangers and cold, heavy air,

I built my kingdom in this forest of despair.

I build my castle of emptiness and sit on my new throne.

This desolate domain is my new home.

Mire of Self-Spite

As I lay my eyes up to the skies,

They stare back with endless dark,

The marsh below mirrors my thoughts,

Is there no respite,

From this pit of self-spite?

The darkness veils my murky mire,

Protecting me from peaceful lights.

Now all that's left is ethereal lights,

From phantom wisps,

That guide my way,

To this mire of self-spite

In creeps the night,

Like the shadow of the moon,

With arms of apathy and voice of gloom,

Smothers me to sleep,

And blankets me with lifeless cold

The mire ashine with flickering lights,

Phantom lights that glow ethereal bright,

Gives my abode an otherworldly sight,

Of an ethereal and unholy night,

In this night I give up my fight,

And bathe in this murky deep.

The Lost Lamb

In a forest dark and vile,

Roams a lamb, pure and white

Lost in the woods with dangers untold,

Yet he goes on, wilful and bold.

In the forest, dark and vile,

Roams a lone wolf full of guile

On the hunt for an easy prey,

A prey that's lost its way.

In the forest, dark and vile,

Lives a spring pure and wide,

Surrounded by trees, wild and green,

Feeds the lives with water clean.

Near a spring pure and wide,

The eyes of the wolf meet the lamb white.

Fate, a cruel and capricious mistress, wolf

With a sadistic smile, her plan she unveils.

Near the spring pure and wide,

The wolf has in his sight a tasty bite.

His eyes gleaming with hunger,

With silent steps, he creeps closer.

Near the spring pure and wide,

Unaware of the plight,

The little lamb drinks away his fears,

Unaware that a spirit of death is near,

His eyes gleaming with intent,

Bloodlust caused by his aromatic scent,

He strides towards his helpless prey,

With a silent pounce, he strikes at his airway.

Crying in terror, blood oozes out,

He turns his head back as he's about to black out

Over him stands the wolf's ghastly shadow.

Forgiving his fate, he departs the deadly meadow.

Smiling ear to ear, he clamps down his jaw,

Extinguishing life with ruthless joy,

"Fate's cruel plans have sent you here to die,

A twisted jest, I can't help but smile."

In the forest, dark and vile,

Innocence succumbs to fate's cruel design.

A lesson for all that can be learned,

Of life's transience and nature's brutal stern.

Forest Fire

In amber flames the forest burns;

Flesh and wood they feed the fire,

Will the departed ever return?

Deer and wolves all flee the flames,

As fear engulfs both predators and preys,

Nature or man, who is to blame?

The fire grows as the forest dies;

The fire denies their final appeal,

Will the earth ever heal?

It all started with a flash,

Now all that's left is ember and ash,

Is saving the earth too much to ask?

A Plea for Peace

She prays for sleep,

A long sleep to end these restless nights.

She prays for peace,

Peace of mind she feels she deprives her kith and kin.

She prays for air,

For the air to escape her lungs, depriving her of life.

She prays for strength,

The strength she needs to put herself in a never-ending sleep.

She prays for rain,

To wash away a stain upon this world.

She prays for the sun,

To shine a light in an empty room,

Once filled with misery.

She prays for the moon,

To shine a comforting light upon her kin.

She prays for the dark,

To engulf her name

Never to be heard again.

She prays for wings,

To carry her away

Beyond the city of lights.

She prays for time

To heal those she left behind,

Mending their hearts with its gentle touch.

Hourglass

Counting grains in the hourglass,
Will they ever stop falling?

How long should I wait,

For this river to dry up?

Or can I walk on water?

I fill this glass with empty words,

And wait for it to be whole

I know where this path leads,

But I'm waiting for time to stop

Close your eyes and count to ten,

Wait for time to stop

I close my eyes and count to ten,

Waiting for time to stop

In Dreams

I tried to see myself in the mirror of life,

All I could see were fading memories.

Now my eyes are sinking,

What was I thinking,

I can't remember the last thing I saw,

I just know that,

I'm dreaming,

This life is just a dream;

Don't wake me up,

Because this song is so soothing,

I hope this lasts forever

I keep telling myself, this is just a dream,

But when I open my eyes,

I forget everything,

I'm lost.

Is this a dream or reality?

I hope,

I'm dreaming,

This life is just a dream;

Don't wake me up,

Because this song is so soothing,

I hope it lasts forever

Now that I'm dreaming,

Don't try to wake me up,

Because I'm gone forever.

End of
WINTER

Echoes of Spring

A songbird sings a sweet melody of a distant spring in the dead cold of winter. Like this songbird, these poems depict sweet tunes of hope in the loud noise of darkness. Let these poems inspire a sense of hope inside you. Even the strongest shackles of despair can be broken by the strength of your resilience.

Symphony of the Moon

In sylvan shade he lays,

Drowned by silence of the night,

The moon gazes upon his face,

A face devoid of happy days

A reflection of days spent without a shadow,

An empty vessel echoing voices from a past spring,

Voices that slowly escape his rusting soul.

Unwilling to watch a star lose its shine,

She starts singing a gentle light,

It dances across the dark skies,

Bathing the night in radiant glow

Creatures of the night, join the tender tune,

The choir of stars sing even brighter so,

The symphony of the night,

Fills his empty soul,

With serene songs of a new spring night.

Now awakened anew,

The moonflower blooms bright.

In sylvan shade he lays,

Bathed in symphony of the night,

The moon gazes upon his face,

A face renewed of happy days,

A reflection of nights spent under the soothing moon;

A vessel echoing songs of a new spring,

Songs that reverberate in his shining soul.

New beginning

Let's grow wings and fly,

We're almost there,

Let's touch the stars,

On our way to glory

We share the same goals,

We share the same scars,

We're all the same

Open the gates,

To a new dawn,

The sun will rise,

Along with a new tomorrow

We've come so far,

Yet it feels so far away,

We've come so far,

We can make to the end,

The sun will rise,

With hope for a new beginning

The skies have changed

They hold the stars,

That brighten the sky

Close your eyes,

It's time to dream,

Open your eyes to a new dawn,

A new beginning

Reshape the clouds,

With your own designs

The gates have opened,

Revealing a new dawn,

The sun has risen,

Heralding a new tomorrow

Hold on to my hand,

I swear this will end

The pain will be gone

Just hold on,

Now open your eyes,

The light has filled the sky

This is a new hope,

This is the new beginning

Home

Far far away,

A place beyond the pines,

Lies an abode,

An embodiment of happiness,

Of peace and serenity,

Of joyful memories,

Beyond the horizon lies my home,

A place of prosperity and beauty,

A paradise to my eyes,

An oasis of tranquillity,

A place to call home,

A place where I belong,

Everyone has a paradise of their own,

A place to call my home,

A place where memories are made,

And where they remain,

Even when you're gone,

Until the end of time,

This is my home,

A palace of memories,

A palace of happiness,

A palace beyond the horizon,

Where the sunrise is beautiful,

And sunset serene.

Formulaic Deconstruction

What is perfection,

Without perception?

A life without meaning,

Deprived of any feeling

The Revelations by the Ancients,

Are encoded within a codex

Confined within the core of our existence

Reevaluate yourself,

Change your vision,

And seek perception,

For that is perfection

The Lockdown

I'm locked down in the dark,

Thinking of giving up hope,

I'm banging and shouting,

Just to get out of here,

Never been so hopeless,

It feels like I'm rotting in hell.

Those without hope,

Never win,

But I feel stronger,

I will get out of here,

From this hell,

This lockdown.

Searching for a way out,

I still don't know why I'm here,

Hope keeps fading,

But then,

A ray of light shines through,

Keeping my hopes up,

Keeping me alive,

It feels like I'm the winner.

Believe

I'm out in the cold,

Miles and mile away from home

I don't know what to do,

Like a child I come to you,

So you can guide my path

When I feel you here,

I feel strong and warm,

You make me feel good,

You trust me like your son,

And that's why I believe in you.

You make me feel safe,

You tend to my wounds,

You mend my broken heart,

The meaning of life,

My comfort and joy

When I feel you here,

I feel strong and warm,

You make me feel good,

You trust me like your son,

And that's why I believe in you.

I give you my heart,

You are my home, my heart, my hearth.

A Melodic Death

Take my hand,

And show me everything in time,

All the memories,

That I try to forget,

Comes back and haunts me,

I tried to find myself,

But the devil tricked me again,

I cannot find myself,

I think I'm lost again

The worst nightmare is over,

Or so I keep telling myself,

But worse is yet to come,

Nothing is short

But then a faint voice,

I'll be there when you know that,

All your hopes are gone,

I'll be there waiting for you,

To call my name.

Panic courses through my veins,

As I see the dark again,

I know not what to do,

Or whom to call out to,

I just keep walking straight,

Trying to find the light

Oh, the devil's here,

He's dragging me to my grave,

But then I see the light,

And I hear the same voice I heard before,

A faint voice,

I'll be there when you know that,

All your hopes are gone,

I'll be there waiting for you,

To call my name.

Shadows

Shadows are a part of you,

They walk beside you, protecting you,

Is it me or is it him,

Who is with you every step,

He walks with you,

Yet you don't realize,

You are not alone,

Every move you make,

You'll never realize,

You are not alone,

He follows your every move,

Protecting you from what you can't fight,

He is your protector.

Through dark valleys when you walk,

When darkness fills your eyes,

He is your light.

When everything turns against you,

And you have nowhere else to turn,

For your aid, he comes,

Yet you don't realize,

You are not alone.

Blue Pill, Red Pill

We're trapped in a world of mirrors,

They hide the truth,

We're mere puppets in this corporate world,

These blinding lights of delusions,

They give false hope,

We live in shadows of thorns,

Open your eyes,

See the truth,

Smash the mirror,

And break free from this world.

Castle of deception,

Built upon lies

Their foundations tremble,

Before your eyes,

The mirrors will disappear,

If you embrace the truth.

Open your eyes,

See the truth,

Smash the mirror,

And break free from this world.

Shattered lies give way,

Now onto a new world,

A world of hope,

A world of truth

Change

Winds of change,

Take everything I have,

Till there's nothing left,

It's time for me to change

I've come this far from my old life,

Never did I listen to a soul,

All this while my hands have been idle,

Now it's time for change,

To leave behind a life of nothing,

And towards something to strive.

Winds of change,

Take everything I have,

Till there's nothing left,

It's time for me to change.

As I break out of my cage,

I think about the difference I can make,

I will lose myself,

And I'll lose my past behind,

I will break myself,

And break my past mistakes,

Now I wait for the winds of change.

End of
SPRING

Summertime Adventures

Warm summer winds call for tales of riveting adventures. You set out on untrodden paths that lead you through sun-drenched meadows, whispering forests that beckon you to explore, sparkling youthful streams, benevolent mountains, and sun-kissed beaches. These poems embrace the spirit of adventure, discovery, and exploration and invite you to witness it.

A Journey Beyond

Yonder he sets his sights,

Away from the flowing Great White,

Memories made, farewells said,

He departs for new waters to tread

Beyond this home, the air is cold,

But greater things are waiting to unfold,

Greener pastures may you find,

If storms arise, you will survive

Travel forth beyond the mountains,

Your promised land awaits,

Fare thee well, oh Black Knight,

Find your fate beyond the Great White

Colours of friendship

They walk along the forest glades,

Through silent trees and sylvan shades,

"I fear these woods and moonlit skies,

By my side will you walk for a while"

With a weary voice he cried,

"Never shall I let go of your hand,

This I promise you my friend,

I shall be with you until the end"

With a voice so bold and filled with pride

As they walk further through the woods,

The forest's deceit unveils,

Through forest traps they proceed,

As night creatures flee.

With the unwavering light of the friend,

They reach the journey's end.

With tearful eyes they depart,

One towards a city bright,

The other towards heavens light.

Oh, dear friend, may you depart in peace,

I thank thee for looking after me,

Even beyond the grave,

Now for you I shall live,

A life fulfilling and brave.

The Lost Son

Shadows swallow whole, a soul wandering adrift.

A nameless boy roams,

Away from home, bereft

Of memories, of hearth

A soul devoid of warmth and care.

Shadow steps he takes across a shallow lake.

A murky, muddy abyss,

That swallows every step he takes.

Yet onward still he strides.

Strange shadows stalk his every step,

Plotting his demise.

Far the distance he spots a sight,

A twisted forest with dangers untold,

Where the songbirds sing a gloomy dirge,

The trees dance a macabre ballet.

Branches like skeletal fingers unfold,

Reaching out to the mourning moon

The air is heavy with a rotting scent.

The wailing winds carry a dire portent.

The forest paths twist and wind,

Creating a twisted maze,

Lost in the haze of this place,

Fear and daze cloud his mind.

Cutting through the leaves, from the skies,

The moon shines a bright

She reaches forth with soothing light,

His fears to subside.

Shines a light through the maze,

Urging him to fight

With every damp step,

He nears the forest's end.

Onward waits a new ordeal,

His path unknown; he has no time to heal.

He ventures forth, towards a misty moor.

A desolate plain shrouded in secret,

By the endless spectral fog

The wind sings a ghastly dirge,

Raising ghostly spectres from the earth

The scent of fear fills the air.

As the veil of uncertainty befalls,

His vision blurred; strange voices he hears

He quests his mouth for a prayer.

Emerged from the mist, dark howling wolves,

Seeking his soul to prey,

Fear grips his legs; his mouth begins to pray.

With a sadistic smile, their fangs they unveil.

Unforewarned, the dirt beneath takes form.

A spectral knight, armour tarnished and worn

The ethereal form speaks with gentle warmth.

"Your journey's end lies beyond the cavern dark,

Seek the light where spring's eternal spark blooms,

Where her gentle embrace awaits."

With these words, he turns his back.

Ready to face a fierce pack.

Yonder in the dark, lit by a burning torch,

The dark cavern yawns

Beholding its gaping maw.

A tunnel to the Everland,

Where every soul must pass.

With a weary soul and dread,

Into the cavern he treads.

He ventures forth, through perilous plight,

Searching for a glimmering shine,

In a dark cavern devoid of light.

A silent tomb with echoes of forlorn days

He bears a burden of immense grief.

A life consumed by endless sorrow.

The cavern cries endless tears,

Partaking in his misery.

In the distance, a glimmering light,

Guiding him by hand,

Towards a land where hope blossoms,

We call it Everland.

Final steps to his journey's end,

To brighter pastures and blooming fields

A realm of eternal spring

Where flowers bloom in comforting light,

Truly a wonderful sight.

A gentle figure, cloaked in serene black,

Awaits him there at the end of his track.

A figure known only to those

Who reach their journey's end.

With pale skin and a heartfelt smile,

She reaches out for an embrace.

Tears stream down his weary face.

As he feels the warmth of the guardian's grace.

A lost son finds his new home,

In the arms that promise rest

With a soothing voice, she proclaims,

"You've travelled so far, my lost son,

Rest now, for your journey is done."

The Hunter and the Healer

Silent as the grave, he moves,

Without contempt or care,

As the world walks,

Through its familiar grooves,

He spreads his fear in the air,

From the unknown,

Comes a healer,

From despair,

Comes a hope,

And thus begins the fight,

Of the hunter and the healer

The hunter spreads his wings of fear,

The skies are dark and bleak,

But the world waits,

With bated breath and prayer,

For hope and a miracle,

From the unknown,

Comes a healer,

From despair,

Comes a hope,

And thus begins the fight,

Of the hunter and the healer

This is a fight for the ages,

This is a fight for power,

This is a fight for tomorrow,

This is a fight for hope

The Hunters Might, The Healer's Plight

As the blanket of night,

Descends upon the wayward woods,

All creatures big and small

In burrows and nests hide.

Arrows fly across the dark skies,

Piercing the curtain of night,

A showcase of the hunter's might,

As the battle intensifies.

Sheltering from the hunter's might,

The healer cowers behind ruins.

Clinging to his life,

He yearns for a way out of his plight.

Inside the ruins sits a wounded wolf,

Bearing its fangs, it's ready to attack.

The healer sits at death's door,

Neither safe in the ruins nor out in the woods.

A situation so dire, yet fear strikes not his heart,

With a bowed head, he approaches the beast.

"Fear not, for I shall heal your wounds."

Hearing these words, the wolf drops his guard.

A healing light descends upon the dying wolf.

He gets up and glances at the healer's face,

Attacks him not for his gracious work.

With a thankful look, he moves towards the woods.

Hours pass as he lies in wait,

Pondering the thought of eternal sleep,

With reassured eyes, he stands up,

Ready to face his awaiting fate.

With a courageous heart, he walks to the woods,

Where a strange new sight awaits.

On the ground lies the hunter, dead.

Above him stands the thankful wolf.

The Architects of Yore

Strike!

The ground and give it form.

Feel the earth rumble.

Arise!

Structures from the ground, take form.

Forged from the void's crucible.

Take shape!

From my dreams, a city of gold,

An empire fit for undying kings.

Behold!

Many a tales yet to unfold,

As they pull these tight-wound strings.

Breathe!

Be sentient, dolls of clay,

Your form inanimate shall be no more.

Beware!

Stay pure or suffer decay,

This a warning from the Architects of Yore.

Hark!

They are the wrath that befalls the reviled

The benevolent winds that blow from yonder,

Decide!

City of dreams, or city of screams, what shall it be?

This I leave you to ponder.

Beyond the Horizon

Face towards the west,

Where the sun sets

Sit back and watch the waves dance,

Under the night sky

Wake up,

This is when we come alive,

Let the wind carry you away,

Away beyond the horizon,

We can walk on water,

As if it were glass.

Silent steps we will take,

Under the cover of darkness,

We walk the path,

To unleash our true potential.

We start from nothing,

To become larger than life.

White World

Far and wide, a world so white,

In name alone, it remains so bright.

We bleed no red,

Our lives are filled with dread.

All colours escape from sight.

I scour alone far and wide.

Through desolate fields, vast and empty,

In search of colour

I must go on,

Venture beyond these vast boundaries.

Through transient rains and hard terrains,

Silent skies and mourning plains,

Our eyes open wide

Towards the end

Behold, a place so bright.

In search of colour, I found a light.

One so bright, it brought back colour

To a world so white,

Now not just in name is bright

For vibrant colours return to sight.

Convergence

Ruptured are the hands of time,

These clocks no longer chime.

Time stands still,

Hoping the void will fill

Memories of a past life,

Flood my mind

Convergence of the multiverse,

The timelines merge

Convergence of dimensions

The timelines merge,

Converge, Create,

Infinite possibilities

People will change,

But these structures remain

Untouched by time,

With future unknown

Open your eyes,

To infinite possibilities

Unknown lies my future,

As the timelines merge

Convergence of dimensions

The timelines merged,

Converged, Created,

Possibilities explored.

End of
SUMMER

Autumn of Reflection

The autumn air carries a sense of longing, reminding me of seasons past. As the leaves change colour and fall, they show me bittersweet memories of a nostalgic past. These are poems from when I first started writing- when everything was simple, and self-doubt was not my constant companion.

Angels

Carry me in your arms,

Dig me straight to the ground

Lift me up to heaven's arms,

And let me in through the gates

Throw me straight to the ground

Don't wake me up from this dream

I'll never lose myself again

For I am dead.

Heaven's angel, evil angel

Sing the anthem of the angels

Am I living or dead,

I don't care anymore.

Broken dreams inside my body,

Don't let me live.

So just kill me now,

I'll live another day.

Don't take me under,

Don't drive me crazy,

Just drive me hard to the gates,

And let me go.

Stranger

I walked past you,

And still, you don't see me

Never listened to a word I said,

Like you don't know me

I ask you again,

If I'm a,

Stranger Stranger,

I'm in danger,

Help me or I'll fall away

Stranger stranger,

Turn away,

Like I'm your enemy

Call my name,

One last time,

Then I'll go away.

Fallen into the dead,

I'm just sleeping here,

Please wake me up,

I'm not your enemy

For one last time

Stranger, Stranger,

I'm in danger,

Help me or I'll fall away

Stranger, stranger,

Turn away,

Like I'm your enemy

Call my name,

One last time,

Then I'll go away.

Please don't treat me,

Like a stranger

If I'm dead,

Just wake me up,

Just pass away

I'm not a stranger.

Dark Shadows

Ever cared to ask me why I'm walking alone?

Did you ever care where I'm going?

Did you ever care why I've been crying?

You'll never know again

Dark shadows,

Are the only one who walks,

Beside mc because,

I'm lonely,

Please walk with me

And I'll never feel alone

I have a long road ahead

It's dark and lonely

Don't mind me, I'm just a passer through,

If you ask me why, I'll explain

Dark shadows,

Are the only one who walks,

Beside me because,

I'm lonely,

Please walk with me

And I'll never feel alone

Walk with me or I will fall,

Fall into the dark.

Voices

I can hear voices,

Deep and dark voices,

They break my silence,

And make me shout,

Kill it, kill it,

The voices in my head,

Kill it, kill it,

The voices in my head,

Just shut up

They won't shut up,

They are breaking my silence,

They whisper in my head,

They drive me crazy

Kill it, kill it,

The voices in my head,

Kill it, kill it,

The voices in my head,

Just shut up

Shut up, shut up

There are voices in my head

Kill it

Shut up, shut up,

There are voices in my head

Just kill it,

Shut up,

That's better.

Intruder

I know it's hard to get you now,

I tried so hard to get you,

But something gets between us

I don't know what to call it

Intruder, Intruder

Why don't you go away

Intruder, Intruder

Why don't you fall away

I just want to talk

So run away, intruder.

The voices in my head,

Are making this too bad

Just go away,

Intruder, Intruder

You are an intruder in my heart,

In my head,

And in my eyes

I tried to stop you,

But you won't stop

Now I'm the intruder in your eyes

The Dead

I'm stuck in the dark side of the world

I'm afraid of my own shadow

I'm waiting for you to rescue me,

From this hell you've dragged me to,

Promising me that you'll rescue me

I can see shadows crawling,

Black clouds thundering,

Dark voices keep asking me,

Can you see me?

Can you hear me?

I will do anything for you,

To take me away from this hell

Let me live

One part off me has died,

Trying to save me from this place,

So we won't share the same fate,

So you can rescue me,

Before it's too late

I can see shadows crawling,

Black clouds thundering,

Dark voices keep asking me,

Can you see me now?

Can you hear me now?

I will do anything for you,

To take me away from this hell

Let me live

I know you will come,

To rescue me,

From the dead.

Hope and Dreams

You are like my shadow,

Everywhere I go I see you,

Everyone I meet looks like you

I see your reflection on the water,

Which slowly fades away.

I can't do this anymore,

I've got to get out of here,

I've got to get out of here right now

I run, run, run away,

From all my hopes and dreams,

Just to find you,

I've got to find you,

Because I can't live without you,

You fade, fade, fade away,

When I get near you.

Why is this happening?

How is this happening?

If it's just a dream,

Just wake me up,

Let me wake up.

You're my only hope and desire,

I just need a way to find you,

You are my brightest day,

Which slowly fades away,

Into the deepest darkness

I hope we meet again.

Name game

Is there something disturbing you?

You've got to name it now,

You've got to tell me now,

This is something that I've been working on

All words and numbers keep confusing me,

I can't stand you anymore,

I can't see my name anywhere.

Now I'm playing the name game,

Blame it on your name,

Because I can't hear it anymore,

I know you are asking for my help,

But I can't hear it anymore.

Now I know why,

You're playing the name game

Everyone wants to see the best in me,

My name is the best part of me,

But I'm no Shakespeare to ask,

"What's in a name?"

Now I'm playing the name game,

Blame it on your name,

Because I can't hear it anymore,

I know you are asking for my help,

But I can't hear it anymore

Now I know why,

You're playing the name game

It's my name, my name,

I'm playing the name game,

My name is where we start,

Now that you know let's start,

Now that I know let's play,

Let's play the name game.

Game of Life

You were my friend,

But you turned against me.

Now you're my for,

Now I'll let you know,

How bad I can be

Your time is up,

Now it's my turn to play

I'm a killer,

I'm going to kill you from the inside,

You're suicidal.

You've lost the game of life

And now there's nothing else you can do.

Or let's move on,

And carry on where we left.

What's it going to be?

Win or lose,

You're going to die,

In this game of life

Broken in the inside,

You need to be fixed

And thing about the future,

Because you're going to pay,

For what you've done

You're broken,

Living in the past,

In the future you will pay.

Painkiller

I'm gonna make a little room for me to feel,

Feel the pain inside, giving me a hard time

The pain is close to my heart,

It is getting painful,

With you far away from me

Come closer to me,

Stay with me

You're my painkiller

With you near me,

The pain goes away

Stay with me until the end.

I'll never feel pain with you near me,

Whenever I think of you the pain goes away,

I know I'm going to die,

But with you near me,

I will die a painless death.

Trouble

Trouble, bored, and disturbed,

That's how I feel right now,

So stay a few blocks away from me,

Because I know you are trouble,

Why don't you try to be interesting,

Right now, I am,

In the corner, far away from you,

I'm not alone here,

I feel a presence here,

Is this a bad omen,

Because I feel troubled again

I've always thought of you as a bad omen,

Just to know it wasn't true,

Now how can I make it up to you.

I knew it then, and I know it now,

And the day to come,

But still, I will think of you as a big trouble,

You are trouble,

And I believe it,

And it won't change

God help me from myself,

Because I am the trouble.

With You

Your face makes me happy,

And that's the reason I'm always happy

You are my lucky charm,

You know that everything I do,

Everywhere I go you're always on my mind.

You make me want to kiss you,

And tell you that I love you,

And I will always be with you until the end.

Even when I'm lost,

I will find my way back to you,

And we will be together forever.

When we were kids,

You said we will be together,

Now that we're grown up,

Our dreams have come true,

Now we are together forever,

Together forever,

I know we'll never fall apart,

Dream on till we die,

This life is a dream,

So let's dream on.

Short Term Memory Loss

I keep asking myself, who am I?

Where am I from? What am I doing here?

I know it's a shame,

But don't blame me,

Because I've got,

Short term memory loss,

I don't know what I'm doing,

I can't remember anything,

I've got short term memory loss,

It's a little sad,

But don't blame me,

Blame my memory.

When I was a young boy,

I tried to climb a tree,

But my hands were too small,

So I fell from a great height,

And now I'm living with,

Short term memory loss,

I don't know what I'm doing,

I can't remember anything,

I've got short term memory loss,

It's a little sad,

But don't blame me,

Blame my memory.

Last night I came back home,

Turned on the gas, and forgot to light it.

And the last thing I know,

My house was in flames,

I'm lying on the ground,

Trying to figure what happened.

Short term memory loss,

I don't know what I'm doing,

I can't remember anything,

I've got short term memory loss,

It's a little sad,

But don't blame me,

Blame my memory.

Grudge

You said you don't miss me,

But I can see it in your eyes,

You miss me very badly,

You tried to act like you don't love me,

But it's too hard to do that,

Because I know you love me

Do you have to do that,

Now that I'm back,

You don't need to worry,

Because I'll never leave you,

Forevermore.

Holding a grudge won't help,

Because the past is over,

You don't need to worry,

Because I'll never leave your side again.

Live It

You know the past is already over,

The future is yet to be written,

But the present is now,

So live it

The present is a gift,

You don't have to worry,

About the future,

That is yet to come,

So live it, live it, live it, it's a gift

Do you think you can write the future?

While dwelling in the past?

So stop worrying and live

The gift is now,

It's your chance to live it,

The gift is now,

Just live it.

Fly

Fly, fly little bird,

To the tower across the mountain,

I'm waiting for the message you carry,

Come on little bird,

You can brave the challenges along the way,

Fly, fly little bird,

Your strong wings can carry you a long way,

You'll save countless lives,

For you,

There's a special place in heaven.

Flying through the storm,

You are God's messenger,

I don't know how you do it,

But the Lord is proud,

Of his great creations like you,

Fly fly,

You can fly a million miles,

For God,

For us,

For countless lives.

Unbeatable

This fight is over,

Let go,

I am the winner,

You underestimate me,

You thought I would lose,

But the fact remains,

I am a winner,

I never lose,

In life and in games,

Face it,

That is the truth,

I am a winner,

I am unbeatable

You thought I was a weak fool,

But the truth is,

I am an ordinary man,

With an aspiration,

To win every battle in life,

To prove,

I never lose

The truth,

A fact,

An aspiration,

To be unbeatable.

The Curse

This was now how it was supposed to be,

Breaking things, destroying places,

Watching loved ones die,

Letting our friends take blame,

When the bad live a strong and rich life,

This is the curse of humans,

To kill, destroy, and burn

But I believe,

When He sees this, he will change,

The curse of humanity

There was a time,

When we all lived in peace and harmony,

Now all that matters is money,

I find this so funny,

Because this is not how we are

Blood money and power,

This is all they want,

If this is a curse,

I believe it will change.

Battleground

Fallen in the warzone,

Tired and weary,

People fighting for their lives,

People lying dead and cold around me,

All I can hear is,

Bang, bang, bang, bang

Never give up,

Never start what you can't finish,

If you cannot complete it, why should I?

You'll never rest,

Never start what you can't finish.

You shout at me for all my mistakes,

All the hatred and jealousy,

You hold against me won't help,

Because face it,

I'm better than you.

It's always about,

You, you, you, you

Never give up,

Never start what you can't finish,

If you cannot complete it, why should I?

You'll never rest,

Never start what you can't finish.

Why did you have to start,

What you can't finish,

You make me sick,

You'll never know,

The feeling of being a winner.

Damnation

I've waited long enough,

I've trained my whole life for this moment,

Will it hurt?

Will I survive?

I don't care, because I'm about to find out,

The pain I caused,

The burden you carried for me

Feel,

I'm ready to feel your pain,

Wait,

I'm waiting for the end,

Feel,

I'm ready to feel the pain I've caused all these years

I've given you nothing,

Nothing but pain all my life,

Will I be forgiven?

Or will I be damned?

Hand of a Friend

I'm your friend,

I'm here to help,

I'm not your enemy,

You have to trust me,

Before it's too late,

Now hold my hand,

And I'll take you to my house.

Don't turn away from me,

It hurts me when you turn against me.

Don't run away from me,

I'm just here to show you the way,

To safety,

To my house.

Why do you hate me?

What did I do to you?

I'm just here to help,

Just take my hand,

And I will keep you safe,

From the devil,

Don't let him take control over you.

Don't turn away from me,

It hurts me when you turn against me.

Don't run away from me,

I'm just here to show you the way,

To safety,

To my house.

Soar into the Sky

Why hide yourself?

Behind the mask,

What are you hiding from?

Has the end of days fallen upon us?

Or are you afraid to face your fears?

Tell me and I can break the mask.

I'll strengthen your wings,

And we will soar into the sky like eagles.

Let me walk inside you,

And silence the storm inside.

Together we'll fly,

And touch the sky.

Fly high, o'child,

I'm right behind you,

Your wings are strong,

Now you will never fall.

Your heart has stopped bleeding,

The wind will carry you now,

Rise from the ashes like a phoenix,

And fly towards the horizon.

Dreamscape

I close my eyes and dream,

Dream of a perfect world,

A world of my creations,

A perfect world,

A perfect design,

Built from my imagination,

Built to perfection,

I will never open my eyes,

I am never leaving here,

I am the contortionist,

I contort shapes to perfection,

I am a creator,

I create a world,

A place where I belong,

There is something inside me,

A hollow space,

Emptiness,

I hope to fill,

To this dying world,

I breathe life,

I bring light to this world,

I fill the void inside,

I am the contortionist,

I contort shapes to perfection,

I am a creator,

I create a world,

A place where I belong,

I am life,

I am light,

I am hope,

I am the contortionist

End of
AUTUMN

Season's End

As the winter chill departs, the lives around transform.

The skies grow black, and the shadows leave a hint of despair.

A faint hue of tranquillity shines through the clearing storm.

As the spring blossoms fade, a mystery fills the air,

Of the roots entwined with a past cold and forlorn.

The winds wipe my tears, with triumph in the air.

As the summer breeze blows away, the past adventures we mourn.

We bid adieu to old chapters, embracing the coming fall.

Golden leaves dance to the wind as they herald in a new morn.

As the autumn leaves fall, the seasons prepare for their curtain
call.

Whispers dance in the breeze, recalling seasons of the past;

I close my eyes and put to rest the golden leaves of the fall.

With one last glance through seasons past,

A peaceful smile fills the sky.

Like clockwork, the cycle is reborn, forever to last.

SEASON'S
End

Thank you for reading.

May these poems find a home in your heart. Until next time.

Instagram: @joelr3d